Andrea Venterra

Car Travel in Italy:
The Insider's Guide to Italian Driving

*How to Navigate Italy's Roads with Confidence and
Drive Like a Local*

MistralBooks

2

To stay in touch and receive a short guide: *Etiquette Tips for Dining in Italy,* visit:
www.mistralbooks.com/andreaventerra
or scan the QR code below

Contents

Foreword

It doesn't matter if you find yourself behind the wheel in Italy for the first time or you're making your annual return to the **land of art, pasta, and perplexing road etiquette,** a concise yet complete guide to the rules of Italian roads might just be the travel companion you're after.

Consider this your easygoing **guide to blending in with the Italian road vibe** – where a subtle head nod might say more than a honk, and finesse means (sometimes) rolling with the chaos rather than fighting it.

For the inexperienced driver in Europe, and in Italy in particular, navigating the continuous **game of "guess the traffic rule"** could feel a bit overwhelming. However, after reading this book, my hope is that you'll feel ready and at ease to enjoy the ride on Italy's picturesque roads.

Before we delve into the details, let me introduce myself. I've traveled extensively, driving in various parts of the world and gathering stories and experiences along the way. Having **lived in both the UK and the US,** I've had the opportunity to explore different corners of the globe. However, after years of wandering, **I've chosen to stay in Italy with my wife and kids.**

Simply put, I'm well-versed in driving in Italy. Whether maneuvering through **bustling city streets in compact cars or navigating highways in family-size station wagons,** I've experienced it all on Italian roads.

So, get ready for **a comprehensive journey through the essentials of driving in Italy.** Consider me your virtual co-pilot, guiding you through the nuances and quirks of Italian driving. ***Happy travels!***

1. – Driving in Italy: To Drive or Not to Drive?

Before you break a sweat over the idea of steering through Italian roads, take a moment to consider **if it's really necessary for your next travel** or holiday.

Consider that If your Italian escapade involves city-hopping, the (almost always...) excellent **bus, train, and metro networks could get you covered.**

Bid "arrivederci" to the stress of city traffic, the parking puzzle, those pesky ZTLs (limited traffic zones), one-way mazes, narrow roads, and pedestrian-packed streets.

On the flip side, **if your plans involve rustic retreats and countryside hideaways,** a set of wheels might be your best bet. Remote villas and snug accommodations may not boast public transport options.

Having your own vehicle grants you the power to halt wherever and whenever the mood strikes. No timetables to adhere to, no rushing for that next train — just you, the open road, and the freedom to explore at your own pace. This option particularly shines if you're toting kids, a horde of passengers, or enough luggage to outfit a small army.

1.1 — Pros vs. Cons: What to Expect

Consider your travel itinerary: evaluate your planned itinerary and destinations to determine whether driving offers logistical advantages. While urban centers like **Rome and Florence may have efficient public transit systems,** accessing rural areas, scenic countryside routes, or remote villages may be more convenient with a car.

Assess the accessibility of tourist attractions, accommodations, and dining options based on your preferred mode of transportation.

Plan for parking: factor in parking availability and costs when considering driving in Italy. In major cities and tourist hotspots, parking can be limited and expensive. Research parking options such as garages, lots, and street parking regulations to ensure hassle-free parking during your travels. Additionally, consider accommodations with complimentary parking facilities to streamline your travel experience.

Navigate traffic and road conditions: be prepared for the unique challenges of driving in Italy, including heavy traffic, narrow streets, and (sometimes) aggressive driving behavior. Familiarize yourself with common traffic patterns, roundabout etiquette, and navigating through historic city centers with restricted zones or limited access. Stay alert, patient, and adaptable to effectively navigate Italian roads and ensure a safe and stress-free driving experience.

Explore Transportation Alternatives: while driving offers flexibility and autonomy, explore alternative transportation options for certain legs of your journey. Utilize Italy's extensive rail network for long-distance travel between major cities and regions. **Consider guided tours,**

bike rentals, or walking tours for exploring urban areas or tourist attractions where driving may be impractical or less convenient.

Summarizing all up:

Advantages of Driving in Italy	Disadvantages of Driving in Italy
Ability to explore multiple destinations	High cost of gasoline/fuel
Flexibility in planning your itinerary	Expensive toll charges
Ample space for luggage	Responsibility for vehicle and damages
Cost-effective for larger groups	Challenges with parking availability and expenses
Convenience for accommodating needs of children (e.g., restroom breaks)	Dependence on public transportation for urban exploration

1.2 – Navigating Italy: To Drive or Not to Drive in Specific Regions

Always consider the terrain, and let's map out which regions beckon you to take the wheel and which ones suggest opting for alternative modes of exploration.

1) Sicily – _Good Choice!_
This incredible island, with its archaeological wonders, countryside escapes, and pristine beaches, is best savored at your own pace. Ditch the train delays and crowds, and embrace the freedom to roam with a rental car.

2) Puglia – _Good Choice!_
Exploring Puglia's charming towns, beaches, and the elusive "trulli" (typical houses) necessitates the convenience of a car. For venturing into neighboring **Basilicata** and the spellbinding **Matera,** having your own wheels is a boon.

3) Piedmont and Wine Rural Areas – _Good Choice!_
To fully enjoy the charming small wine villages such as **Barolo, Alba,** famous for its truffles, **Monforte d'Alba,** La **Morra,** or **Asti** and **Vercelli,** a car is essential. These

picturesque destinations, each with its own unique attractions, are most conveniently explored by car, enabling you to relish the splendor of Piedmont's wine country at your leisure.

4) Tuscany and rural Chianti – _Good Choice!_

Venturing beyond Florence into the rolling hills of Tuscany, with pit stops at **San Gimignano, Volterra, Siena,** and the picturesque **Chianti** region, deserves the freedom that a car provides. Parking amidst vineyards or capturing the essence of charming villages is simply easier on four wheels.

5) Liguria and Cinque Terre – _NOPE!_

The quintet of **Monterosso, Vernazza, Corniglia, Manarola,** and **Riomaggiore** invites exploration sans car. Park your worries in La Spezia and embrace the simplicity of train travel to navigate these enchanting villages.

6) Amalfi Coast – _NOPE!_

Amalfi's **narrow, cliff-hugging roads** are best left to the more adventurous souls. Opt for the scenic buses, boats, and your own two feet to navigate the breathtaking Amalfi

Coast. Taxis, if needed, offer a stress-free alternative for remote adventures.

7) The Dolomites – _Good Choice!_

While the Dolomites boast an efficient public transport system, the allure of freedom to halt at "rifugi" (shelters) or pause for mountain-pass snapshots is undeniable with a car. It's a choice between convenience and the joy of spontaneous detours.

8) Sardinia – _Good Choice!_

If your itinerary veers away from beach-bound retreats, a car proves indispensable for uncovering the mountain villages and hidden gems strewn across Sardinia.

9) Umbria – _Good Choice!_

The quaint villages of Umbria beckon the explorer within. A car unlocks the ability to hop between these gems seamlessly.

10) Friuli – _Good Choice!_

Unveiling its treasures – Aquileia, Cividale del Friuli, and renowned wineries – Friuli shines brightest when you're behind the wheel.

11) Italian Lakes – _Good Choice!_

Embarking on an exploration of the enchanting Italian Lakes? Having a car at your disposal provides the freedom to seamlessly wander between the likes of **Lake Como, Lake Garda, Lake Maggiore, Lake Orta,** and more. Despite being grouped as one 'area,' the distances can be substantial. Whether you fancy the town of **Como,** the allure of Isola Bella, the charm of Stresa, the tranquility of **Orta San Giulio,** or the excitement of Garda's theme parks and water parks, a car unlocks the scenic tapestry of Italian lake vistas.

12) Emilia Romagna – _NOPE!_

In the heart of Emilia Romagna, navigating between main cities like **Bologna, Modena, Parma, Ravenna,** and **Ferrara** is effortlessly achieved by train. While the train network seamlessly connects urban centers, venturing to explore parmigiano cheese producers or car museums (with the exception of one Ferrari museum in Modena) might require a bit more strategic planning. However, the well-established rail system remains a convenient option for city-to-city travel within the region.

Finally, for travelers in search of inspiration for their next adventure, I have curated **a collection of three potential itineraries.** These itineraries are tailored as short excursions by car, traversing the breathtaking landscapes from the northern regions to the southern vistas of Bel Paese.

Each route is meticulously planned to offer a diverse range of experiences, allowing travelers to immerse themselves in the captivating tapestry of Italian sights, sounds, and flavors. **For comprehensive routes and recommendations,** I invite you to explore Appendix A — Three Possible Itineraries.

1.3 — Exploring Italy Beyond the Steering Wheel: Alternatives to Driving

1) Rail Roaming

Train — Italy's veins pulsate with **a well-connected train network,** whisking you (almost always) effortlessly between major metropolises on the "alta velocità" (high-speed) trains and meandering through regional charm on the "regionale" (regional) trains (check here: www.trenitalia.com and here: www.italotreno.it. Please take into account the possibility of strikes ("scioperi") and delays ("ritardi"), especially affecting regional trains. Italian railways often encounter challenges like these, which can significantly impact travelers."

2) Skyward Soaring

For those looking to trim travel time, the skies beckon. Italy's expansive network of airports (have a look here: www.enac.gov.it/aeroporti), coupled with the abundance of low-cost carriers, opens a gateway to swift and often economical flights.

3) Rolling on Rubber

While sometimes **less than ideal for local commutes** (with frequent delays and not an overabundance of bus stops), buses in Italy, such as *FlixBus* (www.flixbus.it), also cover long-distance routes. They provide a **budget-friendly option** for those who are content to gaze out the window as the landscape unfolds."

4) Maritime Musings

Venture away from the mainland and embark on a journey towards Italy's captivating islands – **Sicily, Sardinia,**

Capri, Elba, and many others. A nautical escapade offers a scenic approach to these coastal wonders. However, once on an island, remember that **having a car might still be necessary** to explore its charms fully. For insights into routes and schedules, visit www.traghettilines.it.

5. Chauffeuring

Elevate your travel experience and expenses by engaging a private driver (NCC – noleggio con conducente). While **pricier than self-driving,** it provides an opportunity to recline, unwind, and soak in the scenery without the navigation hassle.

2. – Renting a car in Italy

Renting a car in Italy is a straightforward process if **proper planning is undertaken**, and one arrives at the car rental agency adequately prepared.

When searching for rental options, utilizing a search consolidator such as www.rentalcars.com or www.kayak.com can be advantageous. It is advisable to **compare prices and vehicle availability** on both platforms, as well as checking with individual car rental companies.

Several reputable car rental companies operate in Italy, including but not limited to: Hertz, Budget, Sixt, Alamo, Avis, Europcar, SIXT, etc.

2.1 – The Insurance

In compliance with Italian law, the **Collision Damage Waiver** (CDW) is a mandatory inclusion in the rental rate. It is essential to note that the standard CDW provides only basic coverage, and the deductible can be significantly high, often exceeding € 1.000/1.500 per instance of damage to the vehicle.

For enhanced coverage, individuals have the option to **pay an additional fee** either at the time of booking or during the rental car contract signing to secure a lower deductible or even a €0 deductible.

As of 2024, the cost for a zero deductible plan typically ranges between € 25-50 per day, contingent on the vehicle's size. Various car rental companies employ different nomenclatures for such plans, commonly referred to as 'Zero Deductible' or 'Zero Damage'.

This additional CDW coverage can be **obtained directly from the car rental company** or through an external insurer. Opting for insurance through an external provider requires individuals to pay for damages upfront and subsequently seek reimbursement from the insurance company.

It is essential to note that if you have prior experience renting cars in other countries, where you may have declined automatic insurance or Collision Damage Waiver (CDW) coverage, **the situation differs in Italy. In Italy, CDW is legally mandatory and is automatically incorporated into the car rental rate,** making it non-negotiable.

While some might question the necessity of CDW due to existing coverage through credit card companies, it's crucial to recognize that **in Italy, one cannot decline this insurance.** Despite this legal requirement, it is advisable to contact your credit card company. Many have reported obtaining written and verbal assurances from their credit card companies, guaranteeing coverage for the driver in Italy even when the driver cannot refuse the mandatory insurance.

TIPS&TRICKS – *It's important to be familiar with the terms used in car rental agreements. You will often come across both LDW (Loss Damage Waiver) and CDW (Collision Damage Waiver) on rental websites and contracts. Generally, LDW includes CDW and theft coverage, but it's crucial to carefully read the fine print in your specific contract for clarification. If the contract is not in English (which is quite uncommon, to be honest), make sure to have it properly explained or translated.*

2.2 – Which Car and Where?

Opting for an **automatic transmission whenever possible** is recommended for driving in Italy, especially if you are not already familiar with manual.

While manual transmission vehicles are more common, the **challenges posed by hills, narrow roads, and one-way traffic** make automatic transmission vehicles preferable. Reserving an automatic vehicle in advance, if possible, is advisable to ensure availability.

Improving your car rental experience can be achieved through strategic planning regarding pick-up and drop-off locations. If feasible, you might want to think about **choosing different cities** for these purposes. For instance, if your itinerary involves arriving in Milan and departing from Naples, you could look into **picking up your rental in Milan and returning it in Naples.** However, it's important to be aware of potential extra fees that may come with this choice. While there might be added expenses, the convenience could ultimately outweigh them, especially when considering factors like fuel, tolls, and the value of your vacation time

2.3 – Documents needed

1. Your **driver's license** from your country of residence.
2. An **International Driving Permit** if you're not a European Union resident. Although the rental agency may not always ask for it, it's a legal requirement and might be requested by police during inspections.
3. Your **international identification** (passport).
4. **A credit card** (unless you've made alternative arrangements with the rental company to use a different payment method).

---

*TIPS&TRICKS – A helpful tip to note is that most rental car companies in Italy stipulate a requirement for you to **have held your driver's license for at least one year**. If you have renewed your license within one year of renting a car, it is advisable to bring your old license as a precaution.*

2.4 – What to Do

Performing a comprehensive walk-around inspection when picking up your rental car in Italy is a prudent practice. Instead of simply getting in and driving away, **take the time to thoroughly check the vehicle.** Note any existing dings and scratches on the contract with the rental agent to avoid potential issues later. In Italy, rental cars may exhibit more wear and tear, and it's crucial to ensure that any pre-existing marks are documented before leaving the rental lot. Consider taking a short video of both the interior and exterior of the vehicle for added documentation.

Additionally, inspect the inside of the car to confirm the presence of the legally required safety triangle and safety vest.

In certain regions of Italy, snow tires or **snow chains are mandatory between November 15 and April 15.** Verify whether your rental car is equipped with the necessary winter accessories, especially if you plan to drive during this period.

When **returning the rental car, it is advisable to do so with a full tank of gas** if you picked up and dropped off the car at the same location. In case the option to return the tank empty was chosen, adhere to that agreement.

A notable tip is to be vigilant about the fuel level provided by the rental company. If the car is not supplied with a full tank, **document it with a photo** and, if possible, inform the rental company promptly.

For the return process, while rental companies may encourage a quick drop-off, it is recommended to **have an agent inspect the vehicle and sign off on its condition**. This ensures that any potential damage is acknowledged. It's crucial to return the car when the rental office is open. If you anticipate being late, notify the rental car office in advance, as **many Italian car rental agencies allow a grace period**, typically around 30 minutes.

2.5 – Rental with Kids

Renting a car with children in tow necessitates thoughtful consideration of their safety and comfort, particularly concerning the provision of suitable car seats.

It is advisable to **check with the rental car agency in advance to confirm the availability of age-appropriate car seats** for your children. While most rental companies offer child seats as an optional extra, making reservations early ensures that the necessary safety measures are in place for your journey.

Child safety is paramount, **not only as a legal requirement in Italy** but also as a fundamental aspect of ensuring a secure and pleasant travel experience. Engage with the rental agency to understand their policy regarding child seats, including the types available and any associated costs.

The **ACI or *Automobile Club d'Italia*** (Italian Automobile Club) is a reliable source for obtaining information on Italy's car seat laws, and their provision of information in English facilitates understanding for international travelers.

It is advisable to **review the specific guidelines and requirements** outlined by the Italian Automobile Club, as these regulations may vary from those in your home country. Have a look here: www.aci.it and also at the end of the book in the Appendix B — Drive With Children: Italian Laws.

2.6 – Car seats and how to call them in Italian

There are various types of car seats in Italy, each designated by distinct names based on their specific functionalities. Understanding these terms is crucial for **selecting the appropriate car seat for your child's age** and needs during travel.

1) **"Ovetto":** This term refers to the infant car seat **designed for newborns and small babies,** often resembling a 'little egg'. Its purpose is to provide a secure and comfortable space for the youngest passengers during car journeys.

2) **"Seggiolino Auto":** Described as **the typical car seat,** the "seggiolino auto" is versatile and can be usually installed either in a forward-facing or rear-facing position.

This adaptability ensures its suitability for various age groups and developmental stages.

3) "Rialzo" / "Alzatina" / Booster: The booster seat, known as "rialzo", "alzatina", or simply booster, serves **to elevate the child** for improved visibility and safety during travel. Boosters may feature armrests ("braccioli") and/or a backrest ("schienale"), providing additional support as needed.

Usually the kind of car seat necessary for your vacation in Italy varies according to your child's age, weight, and height.

Group 0+(Ovetto)	Rear-facing	Up to 13Kg
Group 1 (seggiolino)	Rear or Front-facing	9 to 18 Kg
Group 2 (seggiolino)	Front-facing	15-25 Kg
Group 3 (rialzo)	Front-facing	22-36 Kg

As per the regulations, **children under the age of 12 and those with a height below 150cm are required to utilize an appropriate car seat** or booster seat tailored to their height and weight.

Furthermore, the requirement for car seats to be rear-facing until a child reaches **a minimum age of 15 months** underscores the importance of age-appropriate positioning for the well-being of the child during transportation.

2.7. – Rent a car seat or bring your own?

The decision to either rent a car seat or bring your own when traveling to Italy involves considering various factors, each accompanied by its advantages and drawbacks.

Opting for a car seat provided by the car rental agency may raise **concerns about its "history"** and the unfamiliarity for your child. On the other hand, bringing your own car seat ensures your child's comfort but introduces uncertainties regarding its **handling during airport and plane transit.**

If you're traveling by plane with an infant who has their own seat, using a personal car seat on the aircraft is allowed, but **it's essential to inquire** beforehand. Additionally, it's recommended to book in advance if opting to use a car seat provided by the rental agency, as availability may be limited.

Italy adheres to European regulations, specifically **ECE R44 (based on the child's weight) and ECE R129 i-Size (based on the child's height)**. Car seats used in Italy must bear the orange ECE label, and if bringing your own car seat, it must satisfy Italy's legal requirements.

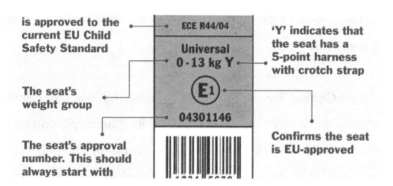

is approved to the current EU Child Safety Standard

ECE R44/04

'Y' indicates that the seat has a 5-point harness with crotch strap

Universal
0-13 kg Y

The seat's weight group

E1

04301146

The seat's approval number. This should always start with

Confirms the seat is EU-approved

Regarding **LATCH/ISOFIX compatibility,** the LATCH system aligns with Italy's ISOFIX system; however, it is essential to confirm the presence of top tethers in rental cars if your car seat requires this feature.

Additionally, **<u>Italy mandates anti-abandonment devices</u>** for children under 4 years old in cars registered in Italy or driven by a resident Italian, whether the vehicle is locally or foreign-registered. Car rental companies often provide these devices, either included with a rented car seat or as a separate rental option. Alternatively, travelers may **bring their own anti-abandonment device** if necessary.

<u>TIPS&TRICKS</u> — If the prospect of bringing your own car seat to Italy is undesirable, and you harbor reservations about the history of car rental company seats, there are alternative options available to ensure the safety and comfort of your child during travel.

One viable option is to purchase a car seat in Italy, thereby addressing concerns related to the unfamiliarity of rental seats. Several avenues exist for acquiring a car seat locally:

1. **<u>Order Online</u>** for Delivery to an Italian Address – Utilize online platforms such as Amazon.it, offering a diverse selection and competitive prices.

2. **<u>Explore nearest Italian baby stores</u>** (search them on Google) like **Prenatal, Chicco, IperBimbo,** and **Bimbostore,** which also provide online purchasing options.

---

3. – The International Driving Permit

Regardless of your origin, if you plan to drive while visiting Italy, obtaining an **International Driving Permit (IDP)** is a mandatory requirement. **Non-European Union (EU) drivers are legally obligated to carry an IDP** alongside their valid driver's license. While it is also possible to have a legal Italian translation of your driver's license, this process is typically more cumbersome and expensive.

If you possess a driver's license **from a European Union (EU)** country, you are exempt from the requirement of obtaining an IDP. EU license holders can utilize their EU license for driving in Italy.

It is crucial to clarify that the term **'International Driving Permit' (IDP) is distinct from an 'International Driver's License'.** The IDP is not a license; rather, it acts as a translation of your driver's license for the convenience of foreign authorities.

Italy, like many other countries, **adheres to the Convention on Road Traffic signed in Geneva in 1949** and also to the **1968 Vienna Convention.**

It's useful to remember this if you are asked which "type" of permit you need when driving in Italy. The "Geneva" permit is valid for 1 year, while the "Vienna" permit is valid for 3 years."

TIPS&TRICKS — Each country has a different procedure for obtaining the International Driving Permit: typically, the procedure is entrusted to the national Automobile Clubs. Here are some examples:

<u>USA</u> — The U.S. State Department exclusively authorizes the **American Automobile Association (AAA)** to sell International Driving Permits (IDPs) to U.S. drivers. The IDP can be acquired through AAA either by visiting a AAA office in person or by mailing the necessary documentation to a AAA office. Info here: www.aaa.com/vacation/idpf.html

<u>UK</u> — Even after Brexit, you **won't need an International Driving Permit** (IDP) for driving in Italy. However, it's advisable to stay updated on any changes or updated news regarding driving requirements. Always refer to the official government website for the most accurate and up-

---

to-date information: https://www.gov.uk/driving-abroad/international-driving-permit

AUSTRALIA – The **Australian Automobile Association (AAA)** is the only authorized distributor for IDPs in Australia. State and territory motoring clubs process them on behalf of the AAA. In NSW the motoring club is the NRMA. For all the details visit: www.aaa.asn.au/international-motoring/international-driving-permits

CANADA – You need to contact the **Canadian Automobile Association** for a Canadian International Driving Permit application form. Official website: www.caa.ca/services/travel/international-driving-permit

4. – Navigating the Roads: Gps and Devices

Navigating the roads in Italy requires a thoughtful approach, utilizing a combination of tools to ensure a smooth and efficient travel experience. The following are recommended tools for navigating Italian roads.

1. GPS Devices

GPS devices, often standard in rental cars or available as an add-on option, provide real-time navigation assistance. However, it is advisable to **exercise caution and not rely blindly on their directions,** as occasional inaccuracies may arise, especially **on Italian country roads** or in small towns, leading drivers down one-way roads or into restricted zones.

2. Google Maps

Google Maps stands out as a reliable and frequently **updated navigation tool in Italy**. It offers comprehensive maps and directions, making it a preferred choice for many travelers. Nevertheless, similar to GPS devices, **users should remain attentive and cross-reference directions** to avoid potential pitfalls such as limited traffic zones (ZTL – see dedicated Chapter).

3. Physical Maps

Traditional physical maps serve as **a valuable backup** and can be particularly useful in areas with limited connectivity or for a broader overview of the route. While technology is prevalent, having a physical map on hand can be advantageous in certain circumstances.

It is essential to be aware that in Italy **speed limits displayed in Google Maps or in other navigation app may not always be accurate.** Therefore, travelers should prioritize adherence to general speed limit rules, unless otherwise indicated by road signs

---

TIPS&TRICKS – Among all navigation systems, however, I see every day that one in particular is commonly used by Italian drivers. **It is the Waze app.** Waze is a mobile navigation app designed to assist drivers in finding optimal routes and provides users with up-to-date information about road conditions, accidents, police

---

presence, and other hazards. I like it because **Waze allows users to contribute to the community** by reporting incidents, hazards, and other information to help improve the accuracy of its data. Using information taken from various sources, **I think it is one of the most reliable** navigation apps in Italy and very well updated.

5. – Italian Driving Laws: A General Overview

Understanding and adhering to Italian driving laws is crucial for a safe experience on the roads. Here are **some key general laws to keep in mind** in addition to what has been already said about child seats, etc. Other laws and regulations are also widely discussed in the next chapters.

1. Right Turns on Red Lights

It is **illegal to turn right on a red light** in Italy. Drivers are required to wait for a green light before making a right turn.

2. Seatbelt Usage

Seatbelts **are mandatory for occupants** in both front and back seats if the vehicle is equipped with them.

3. Headlights Usage

When driving outside of urban areas in Italy, it is **a legal requirement to have headlights on.** Many drivers find it practical to keep their headlights on at all times for increased visibility and safety.

4. Traffic Circles (Roundabouts)

Traffic circles play a crucial role in maintaining the flow of traffic. An Italians really love them. Drivers should **yield to cars already inside the traffic circle** before entering. When exiting, move to the outside lane and use the signal to indicate your intention. If a mistake is made, it is acceptable to navigate the traffic circle again.

5. Intersections and Right of Way

At intersections, the general rule is to **yield to the car on the right.** Always. If in doubt, well... Yield all the same.

6. Mobile Phone Usage

Texting while driving or holding and using a **phone is illegal in Italy.** Hands-free devices are permitted, promoting safer communication while operating a vehicle.

7. Alcohol Limit

The legal blood alcohol limit in Italy **is 0.05% or 0.5 grams per liter of blood,** which isn't much. Enjoying too many glasses of Chianti could put you over the limit. That's why it's important to plan responsibly, like having a designated driver or using alternative transportation, to make sure you stay within legal limits.".

6. – Italian Driving Laws – Types of Roads and General Speed Limits

Road Type	Equivalent in English	Speed Limit	Remember
Autostrada	Toll Motorway	130	110 in poor weather conditions
Strada Extraurbana Principale	Major Highway	110	90 in poor weather conditions
Strada Extraurbana Secondaria	Minor Highway	90	80 in poor weather conditions
Strada Urbana	Urban Road	50	
Strada Bianca	Dirt or Gravel Road	posted limit	

The Autostrada, identified by roads beginning with an 'A' such as A1, spans the length of Italy and operates as a toll road. All signage for the Autostrada is marked in green.

Upon entering the Autostrada, drivers must stop at the barrier to obtain a ticket (biglietto) or pass through the telepass lane without stopping (indicated by yellow markings).

It's essential to note that access to the telepass lane requires a telepass device. However, telepass devices are no longer available as an add-on option with car rentals. If driving a vehicle from another European country, it's advisable to verify compatibility with toll devices beforehand.

Upon exiting the Autostrada, toll payment is required. Drivers can choose between white lanes for cash payment, blue lanes for credit card payment, or yellow lanes for telepass users. Cash and credit card payments involve stopping at the barrier, although many toll booths now offer contactless payment options. With telepass, drivers can pass through without stopping, with a 'beep' indicating successful charging.

In the event of any issues at the entrance or exits of the Autostrada, drivers can seek assistance by pushing the 'help' button. It's crucial never to enter the Autostrada without obtaining a ticket (unless equipped with a telepass device).

Left to right: white lane for cash payment, blue lane for credit card payment and yellow lane for telepass users.

7. – Road Signs

Understanding Italian road signs is crucial for safe and compliant driving. Here is a brief guide on how to interpret Italian road signs based on their shapes and colors.

SHAPES

1) Circular Signs

They indicate either something is forbidden or compulsory. For example:

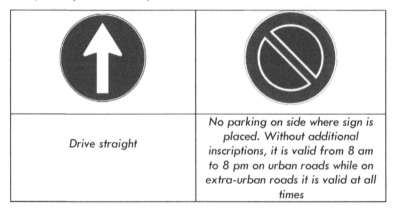

Drive straight	*No parking on side where sign is placed. Without additional inscriptions, it is valid from 8 am to 8 pm on urban roads while on extra-urban roads it is valid at all times*

2) Rectangular or Squared Signs

Serve as informational signs, providing guidance or information about the road. For example:

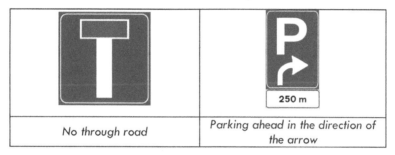

No through road	*Parking ahead in the direction of the arrow*

3. Triangular Signs:

Warn drivers about potential hazards or conditions. If the triangular sign has a yellow background, it indicates a temporary warning. For example:

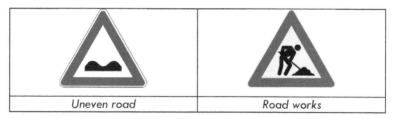

Uneven road	*Road works*

COLORS

1) Green Signs

Typically reserved for highways (Autostrada), which are toll roads. For example:

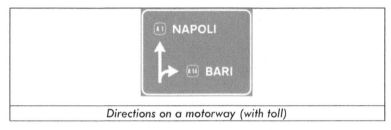

Directions on a motorway (with toll)

2) Blue Signs

Indicate non-toll roads and general information. If they are blue signs with a round or circle shape though they are mandatory signs. For example:

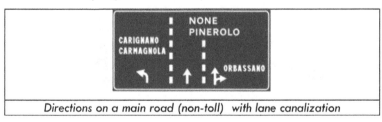

Directions on a main road (non-toll) with lane canalization

3) Brown Signs

Commonly associated with historic or tourist attractions. For example:

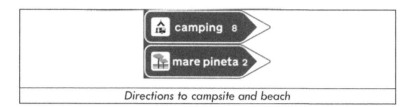
Directions to campsite and beach

Remember to consider **both the shape and color of the road signs** to accurately interpret their meaning.

Please refer to **APPENDIX C** – **for a more detailed list of Italian road signs** and their meaning.

8. – The AUTOVELOX

"Autovelox" is the (unusual) **Italian word for speed camera**. Italian law mandates the **presence of warning signs** indicating an upcoming speed camera. These blue signs (or sometimes white ones – unfortunately, there's no complete uniformity) serve as an alert to drivers, notifying them of the impending enforcement zone.

There is **a 5% leeway allowed** in speed limit enforcement. For instance, if the posted speed limit is 130 km/h, a fine will be issued only if the vehicle travels at speeds over 136 km/h.

And if you're still worried about getting caught, modern technology has your back. Apps (like Waze or others) can **alert you about speed cameras** in real-time, so you can adjust your speed accordingly.

Failure to comply with speed limits can **result in steep fines**. And don't think you are exempt from paying just because you've rented the car.

The rental company will charge your credit card even when you are safely back home if a fine arrives. Nobody wants **a souvenir ticket from their vacation,** right?

Some of the most common Autovelox warning road signs

9. – The SAFETY TUTOR

The Autostrada, Italy's highway network, features **an additional speed limit** monitoring system known as the "**Safety Tutor**" (Italian authorities have a penchant for evocative names, it seems).

Operating between designated points A and B, the Safety Tutor captures the license plate of vehicles and **calculates their average speed** within this interval. If the average speed exceeds the prescribed limit, taking into account the 5% leeway, drivers are subject to fines.

Covering over 2500 kilometers of Autostrade, the Safety Tutor network expands annually. It is mandatory for **signage to indicate the presence of a Safety Tutor** at least 250 meters before its actual location and also up to 4 kilometers before its activation begins.

While the Safety Tutor system often prompts **complaints from Italian motorists,** its implementation has coincided with a significant decrease in driving-related fatalities in Italy.

It's important to note that during **rainy conditions,** the speed limit on the Autostrada **decreases by 20 kilometers per hour,** and the Safety Tutor adjusts accordingly.

Moreover, similar systems measuring average speed are becoming **increasingly prevalent on regular roads.** Therefore, be mindful of signs similar to the ones below:

Signs indicating the presence of a Safety Tutor

10. – ZTL or Zona a Traffico Limitato

In Italy, a ZTL, or **Zona Traffico Limitato,** also known as a Limited Traffic Zone, serves the purpose of **reducing traffic,** congestion, and pollution in city and town centers while promoting pedestrian-friendly environments.

ZTLs may be 'attivo' (active) 24 hours a day, or only during specific hours of the day or certain days of the week. During active periods, **only vehicles with authorization are permitted to enter the ZTL.**

Unauthorized entry into an active ZTL triggers cameras at entry points to **capture photos of the vehicle** and its license plate, resulting in the imposition of fines.

Signs warning of ZTL

Fines for ZTL infractions typically range **from €100 to €350,** in addition to administrative fees. The exact fine amount varies depending on the city in which the violation occurs.

Determining whether your vehicle has permission to enter a ZTL involves understanding specific criteria and exceptions. Typically, vehicles with authorization to enter a ZTL include those owned by **residents, workers, hotel guests,** and individuals utilizing parking garages. Additionally, in certain cities, electric vehicles may have unrestricted access to ZTLs.

It's important to note **that if a ZTL is open, or 'non attivo,' permission is not required for entry**. This distinction simplifies navigation for drivers during periods when ZTL restrictions are not in effect.

The operational hours of ZTLs, indicating when entry is restricted without permission, are typically displayed on a sign prior to the commencement of the zone. Most ZTLs, especially in large cities, **feature a red or green light indicator** or a digital display reading 'VARCO ATTIVO' (active) or 'VARCO NON ATTIVO' (inactive), aiding drivers in making informed decisions. If the indicator is red or 'ATTIVO,' entry is prohibited. Conversely, if it's green or 'NON ATTIVO,' vehicles may enter freely, unless otherwise specified (although this rarely impacts rental cars).

Moreover, if a vehicle enters a ZTL during 'NON ATTIVO' periods, **it may remain within the zone indefinitely**, provided it is legally parked. However, finding parking can be challenging, as most spaces are designated for residents only. While there are no ZTL cameras at exit points, accidentally entering another ZTL during active hours will result in fines.

Lastly, it's crucial **not to rely solely on navigation apps or GPS devices** for ZTL information, as they may inadvertently route drivers through restricted zones. Vigilance and attentiveness to ZTL signs are paramount for avoiding violations.

If your **hotel is situated within a ZTL,** you have the option to request that your vehicle's number plate be registered with the local authorities for the duration of your stay. This registration process is typically **offered free of charge by hotels,** but it's advisable to verify this with your chosen accommodation prior to your trip.

It's important not to enter the ZTL until this registration has been completed. Additionally, even if your hotel allows vehicular access within its ZTL, this **authorization does not extend to all ZTLs in the city.** Therefore, caution should still be exercised to avoid inadvertently entering other restricted traffic areas.

11. – Refueling in Italy

In Italy, gas stations offer **both self-service** ("fai da te") and **full-service** ("servito") options for refueling vehicles.

While opting for full-service may incur slightly higher costs (with prices clearly displayed), it provides convenience as attendants typically **accept payment at the pump,** allowing for a swift departure.

When refueling your vehicle in Italy, it's important to **select the correct type of fuel:** *gasolio* (diesel) or *benzina* (gasoline).

Gas prices in Italy can vary, with **current rates around €1.88 per liter** (*March 2024*), equivalent to approximately $7 per gallon.

However, prices are known to vary greatly, and you could expect anything in the future from €1.50 to €2.00 or more.

Despite the higher prices, **petrol stations are readily available throughout the country**, including small towns, cities, and along the Autostrada, allowing for convenient access without exiting the highway. Even if Autostrada's fuel stations are generally much more expensive than others.

While petrol stations may not operate 24/7, many are **equipped with self-service payment machines** to facilitate refueling during off-hours. Customers can insert Euro bills or cash into these machines, select their pump, and proceed with refueling.

It's essential to choose **the option for a receipt** ("ricevuta") before starting the pump. If payment exceeds the fuel amount, the machine will issue a receipt with the remaining balance, which can be used for future purchases.

For convenience, it's advisable to use small bills or **a credit card for payment**, especially if you won't return to the area.

It's worth noting that **if you opt to rent an electric car** in Italy, you can utilize various apps to locate the nearest electric charging stations, known as "colonnina elettrica".

Some of the widely used apps for this purpose include *NextCharge, PlugShare, EVWay, Chargemap,* and *Emobitaly.*

These apps provide **real-time information on the availability and locations of electric charging columns,** facilitating convenient and efficient recharging of electric vehicles during your travels in Italy.

Fuel in Italian	Fuel in English	What Youl'll find on the Pump
Gasolio	Diesel	Black or blue or yellow label; *Gasolio.* Symbols: *B7, B10, XTL*
Benzina	Gas/Petrol	Green label; *Benzina, Senza Piombo, Senza PB, Benzina Verde.*

Fuel in Italian	Fuel in English	What Youl'll find on the Pump
		Symbols: *E5, E10, E85*

TIPS&TRICKS — When at the pump, you may encounter options for "**metano**" (methane) and "**GPL**" fuel (LPG, *Liquefied Petroleum Gas*), which are not so uncommon in Italy. Disregard these and concentrate on gasolio or benzina, as rental cars are never available in methane or LPG versions.

12. – Parking in Italy

Parking in Italy may present more challenges compared to your home country due **to tight spaces and increasingly larger vehicles.** Additionally, navigating narrow one-way streets with a line of cars behind you while deciphering the fine print on parking signs can be stressful.

However, with some preparation and understanding of parking sign translations, you can confidently navigate parking in Italy and **minimize the risk of receiving a fine** ("multa").

In Italy, parking options can vary between paid and free, with distinct guidelines to follow for each:

1. Free Parking – Parking spaces marked with **WHITE paint or unmarked areas** typically indicate **free parking.** However, it's essential to remain vigilant for signs indicating parking time limits or requirements for parking discs ("disco orario" see also below).

Also, be mindful that in some cities (Florence, for example), in certain areas, **white lines are not free but reserved for residents** (ZCS "Zona a controllo sosta" – controlled parking area). You need to check, especially in city centers, and double-check vertical signs, in order to avoid mistakes.

2. Parking Discs – When parking in areas with **time restrictions,** use a parking disc to indicate the time you started parking. Nearby signs will specify the duration allowed for parking in the space.

3. Paid Parking – In tourist areas and locations marked with **BLUE lines on the pavement,** parking is **typically paid.** Drivers must use parking meters to make payments, which can be done using coins or credit cards. Many parking meters may require input of your license plate information.

Using **apps for parking payments** is also becoming increasingly popular in Italy, so check on parking meters if any QR codes are displayed or if any parking app is advertised to simplify your experience.

After paying for parking, **display the small ticket or receipt from the meter on your front windshield** to indicate valid parking. Ensure to adhere to the hours of operation specified on the meter.

Be especially mindful of parking regulations and avoid parking in prohibited areas, **such as in front of garages, driveways, or in bus or taxi loading zones.** If you see the writing **"Passo carrabile"** do not park there, as it is an area in which cars can be forcibly removed or towed away.

"Passo carrabile" sign: avoid parking!

4. Other kind of lines – **PINK Lines** are relatively rare and usually found in major cities like Rome, Milan, and Florence. These lines indicate **parking spots reserved for pregnant women or new mothers with infants.**

GREEN Lines designate parking spots **reserved for electric vehicles** (EVs). These areas are usually equipped with charging stations to accommodate EVs while they recharge.

YELLOW lines serve multiple purposes. They indicate restricted parking areas, **loading zones, and spots reserved for disabled people.** Parking in these areas without proper authorization or for purposes other than intended can result in fines or penalties.

Parking in all these spots without proper authorization can result in fines or penalties.

Parking in Italy – Words to Remember

A pagamento	Paid parking
Biglietto	Ticket
Corsia	Lane
Disco orario	Parking disc
Giorni feriali	Workdays (Monday to Saturday)

Giorni festivi	Holidays (Sundays and holidays)
Gratuito	Free
Multa	Fine
Parcometro	Parking payment machine
Passo carrabile	Do not park – Risk of being towed away
Solo autorizzati	Authorized only
Solo residenti	Residents only

13. – When Trouble Strikes: Handling Accidents and Automotive Issues

While on vacation in Italy, experiencing **car trouble or accidents** can unfortunately disrupt your plans. However, if you're using a rental car, such issues are often rare, as rental companies typically provide newer vehicles that undergo regular maintenance checks.

1. CAR BREAKDOWNS – In the event of car trouble, it's crucial to prioritize safety. Activate your emergency lights and **maneuver your vehicle to the side of the road,** aiming to completely clear it if feasible. Once parked, don your safety vest and place the safety triangle behind your vehicle, ensuring it's visible to oncoming traffic. Maintain a distance of at least 50 meters from your car, extending to **100 meters if on the Autostrada.**

Seeking roadside assistance is the next step. **You can reach out to the ACI (Automobile Club d'Italia) by dialing 803.116.**

Their services include coordinating towing assistance, though it's important to note that towing expenses typically fall on the vehicle owner.

Alternatively, on the Autostrada, you'll find **yellow call boxes positioned approximately every 2 kilometers,** which provide a means to request assistance. Some rental car agreements may also include roadside assistance coverage.

2. CAR ACCIDENTS – In the unfortunate event of a car accident, following a procedure akin to that of a breakdown is necessary. Immediately contact the Italian police by **dialing the general emergency number, 112.** This number is used also **for calling ambulances.**

Gathering information from involved parties and witnesses is crucial. **Ensure to obtain personal details** and statements, although obtaining cooperation from Italians might prove challenging due **to potential language barriers** and the intricate legal process involved. If in doubt, **do not**

hesitate to call the Carabinieri or Polizia Municipale by reaching them **through the 112 number.**

Documenting the scene with photographs of vehicles, license plates, and relevant surroundings is vital for insurance and legal purposes. Additionally, promptly notifying the rental car company of any damage incurred during the accident is advisable to facilitate the claims process.

TIPS&TRICKS – **"Constatazione amichevole"** is an Italian term commonly used to refer to an amicable settlement or friendly settlement in the context of road accidents. It's a procedure where drivers involved in a minor accident mutually agree on the circumstances and responsibility for the collision **without involving law enforcement or insurance companies.** During a "constatazione amichevole", both parties fill out **a standardized form detailing the accident's circumstances,** including the date, time, location, and a brief description of what happened. Each driver then signs the form, acknowledging their agreement on the accident's details. This document can later be used to support insurance claims or legal proceedings if necessary. The "constatazione amichevole" is commonly used in Italy and some other countries to streamline the resolution of minor accidents, especially when there are no serious injuries or disputes over liability. However, it's important to note that **it may not be suitable for all situations, such as accidents involving significant damage or injuries,** where legal or insurance involvement

---

may be necessary. **As previously said, when in doubt call 112.**

13.1 – Beware of Road Crimes

Italy is **not a particularly dangerous country**. General statistics show this, and violent crimes are quite rare. However, traveling **in Italy is no different from traveling anywhere** else in the world, and it's always wise to be aware of the possibility that someone with ill intentions may try to take advantage of a tourist or traveler.

Therefore, it's advisable to exercise the same common sense and take the same precautions that one would normally take in their own country, even when in Italy.

Below, I will list **some situations that are not specific to Italy** but that sometimes (very rarely actually) can occur here.

I want to emphasize that **thefts or attempted thefts are not "typical" of Italian roads,** but they can happen anywhere.

1) SIDE MIRROR SCAM – *"La truffa dello specchietto"* translates to "the scam of the side mirror". It refers to a common scam tactic where **a perpetrator manipulates a situation involving a vehicle's side mirror** to deceive the driver and extort money or valuables from them.

Typically, the scam unfolds when the perpetrator **deliberately creates a minor collision** or pretends that the victim's vehicle has damaged theirs. They may claim that the victim's car hit their side mirror, even if no contact occurred.

In some cases, they might even intentionally damage their own vehicle to make the situation seem more convincing. Once the victim is convinced or distracted, the scammer **pressures them into paying for the supposed damages** or demands compensation on the spot. This type of scam often targets tourists or individuals unfamiliar with local driving customs and laws, making them more vulnerable to manipulation.

To avoid falling victim to "la truffa dello specchietto" and similar scams, it's crucial to **remain cautious and skeptical in such situations.** Always assess the situation carefully, take note of any inconsistencies, and be aware of your surroundings. If you suspect foul play or feel uncomfortable, **it's always best to contact local authorities** or law enforcement for assistance.

2) A FLAT TIRE? – In the event that someone attempts to flag you down or **signals from their vehicle** that there is an issue with your car, exercise caution as they may be attempting to deceive you. If possible, **proceed carefully to a gas station** or a populated area before stopping. Criminals often aim to lure drivers into secluded areas to facilitate robberies.

3) AT THE GAS STATION – While refueling your vehicle at a gas station, **be cautious if someone approaches you with a question.** Their accomplice may take advantage of the distraction to access your car, possibly opening the passenger door to steal valuables such as a purse or wallet. Especially **if you are alone,** always ensure that your doors are locked and valuables are kept out of sight in such situations.

4) TRUNK/BOOT: CAR SAFETY IN GENERAL – Simply **hiding valuables in your car** may not provide sufficient protection, even though it's the most basic form of safeguarding recommended. It's wise to **avoid leaving**

valuables unattended in your vehicle, especially when checking out of accommodations or making brief stops.

If you need to store luggage in the car, consider having someone **watch over the vehicle** at all times or utilize a left-luggage service offered by hotels or train stations. If leaving your luggage inside the car is unavoidable, ensure that you **keep with you anything that is vital or precious**. While in Italy occurrences of broken windows or forced-open boots are not extremely common, they're not unheard of either.

14. – Etiquette Behind the Wheel: Unveiling Italy's Spoken and Unspoken Rules

Driving in Italy **can be quite an adventure** especially if it is your first time there. Adjusting to the driving culture in Italy requires understanding a few key points:

While generally correct, sometimes **Italian drivers tend to view rules and regulations more as loose guidelines** than strict mandates.

It's not so uncommon to witness drivers zooming through pedestrian crossings, speeding on various types of roads, performing quick "pauses" rather than complete stops at stop signs, and parking wherever they find space.

Confidence and assertiveness are essential qualities for driving in Italy, as hesitancy can lead to difficulties navigating the roads.

In Italy, it's not uncommon to encounter **drivers who engage in tailgating, especially in the "Autostrada"**. However, it's important not to take it personally. Instead, simply **shift to the right into the next lane,** or on narrower roads, pull over momentarily to allow the vehicle to pass safely.

Contrary to some driving cultures, **road rage is relatively rare in Italy**. While you may encounter **colorful hand gestures** or hear some vocal expressions from other drivers, intimidating road confrontations are not a typical occurrence in daily driving experiences.

The **winding nature of many Italian roads** can sometimes lead to particularly difficult exchanges: be prepared to stop and eventually let the other vehicle pass before you, to avoid any discussion on who has or does not have the right of way.

When driving in the countryside, **it's common to encounter cyclists,** who may sometimes ride in large groups despite the legal requirement to ride only two abreast. If you find yourself unable to pass safely, **consider giving a friendly toot of your horn** as a gentle reminder.

While it can be frustrating to be delayed behind a group of cyclists, it's important to remember **that cycling holds significant cultural importance in Italy.** Before attempting to overtake unsafely, try to empathize by imagining one of the cyclists as a loved one, such as your daughter, father, or friend.

If you notice an oncoming driver flashing their lights, it's not a signal that your own lights are off. Rather, **it's a warning that there may be traffic police or a speed trap** ahead, allowing you to adjust your driving accordingly.

Similarly, if a driver **behind you flashes their lights, it's an indication that they intend to pass you quickly.** Signal and move over to the right lane as soon as it's safe to do so. It's advisable to avoid lingering in the left lanes unless actively passing slower vehicles.

In Italy, **overtaking on the right is considered illegal and unexpected** by other drivers. While frustration with slow-moving vehicles in the left lane may tempt some drivers to overtake on the right, it's best to adhere to local customs and regulations.

Compared to driving norms in other countries, Italians may be **less inclined to stop for pedestrians at crosswalks** and more inclined to adopt creative parking solutions, potentially converting two-lane roads into makeshift multiple lanes.

Expect **mopeds to weave in and out of traffic** lanes. Rather than worrying about their movements, maintain your course, and they will (hopefully) navigate around you accordingly.

Lastly, Italy has **a fondness for traffic circles, or roundabouts,** as they are commonly known. When utilized correctly, roundabouts effectively keep traffic flowing smoothly. The key to navigating roundabouts in Italy is to always yield to traffic entering the roundabout. Once inside, it's advisable to **move into the outer lane if you intend to exit** the roundabout. Additionally, signaling your intentions with your turn signals is essential for communicating with other drivers and ensuring safe maneuvering within the roundabout.

Appendix A – Three Possible Itineraries

Embarking on **a road trip across Italy** presents a plethora of possibilities, each promising a unique blend of scenic beauty, cultural richness, and gastronomic delights.

While there are countless routes to explore, we present **three exemplary itineraries** that showcase the diverse charms of Italy's regions, traversing from the lush landscapes of the north to the sun-kissed shores of the south.

In crafting these three exemplary itineraries, we aim to provide a glimpse into the rich tapestry of experiences that Italy has to offer. Whether you're drawn to the culinary delights of **Piedmont,** the artistic treasures of **Tuscany,** or the cultural heritage of **Sicily,** each region promises a journey of discovery and delight. So pack your bags, hit the open road, and prepare to embark on the adventure of a lifetime in bella Italia.

Piedmont Panorama: A Road Trip Itinerary

Piedmont, nestled in the **northwest corner of Italy,** is a region of stunning landscapes, rich history, and unparalleled culinary experiences. Embarking on a road trip through Piedmont offers the opportunity to explore charming towns, rolling **vineyards,** and majestic **mountains** at your own pace.

We'll outline a hypothetical itinerary for a memorable journey through the picturesque region of Piedmont.

Day 1: Arrival in Turin

Start your Piedmont adventure in the **historic city of Turin,** the region's capital. After arriving at the airport, pick up your rental car and check into your accommodation in the city center. Spend the day exploring **Turin's elegant boulevards, grand squares, and world-class museums.** Don't miss iconic landmarks such as the **Mole Antonelliana,** the **Royal Palace** of Turin, and the **Egyptian Museum,** home to one of the most extensive collections of Egyptian artifacts in the world.

Day 2: Turin to Alba

On day two, depart from Turin and head southeast towards the town of **Alba**, approximately **80 kilometers** away. Along the way, consider making a stop in the picturesque town of **Bra** to visit the renowned **Slow Food headquarters**. In Alba, explore the historic center, known for its medieval towers, cobblestone streets, and gourmet food shops. Indulge in the region's famous **white truffles** and **Barolo wine**, and visit nearby vineyards for tastings and tours. Spend the night in Alba or nearby.

Day 3: Alba to Asti

Continue your journey through Piedmont to the charming city of **Asti**, approximately 40 kilometers from Alba. Along the way, consider a detour to visit the hilltop town of **Barolo**, famous for its prestigious wine production. In Asti, explore the historic center, known for its medieval towers, Romanesque churches, and lively piazzas. Don't miss the opportunity to sample **Asti Spumante**, a sparkling wine produced in the region, and indulge in traditional Piedmontese cuisine at local trattorias. Spend the night in Asti.

Day 4: Asti to Lake Maggiore

Depart from Asti and travel northwest towards **Lake Maggiore**, approximately **160 kilometers** away. En route, consider a stop in the town of **Novara** to explore its historic center and visit the impressive **Basilica of San Gaudenzio**. Upon arriving at Lake Maggiore, relax and unwind on the shores of the lake, take a boat cruise to the **Borromean Islands**, and visit the charming town of **Stresa** with its lakeside promenade and botanical gardens. Spend the night in a lakeside hotel overlooking the water.

Day 5: Lake Maggiore to Turin

On your final day in Piedmont, depart from **Lake Maggiore** and travel back to **Turin**, approximately **130 kilometers** away. Along the way, consider a stop in the town of **Ivrea** to visit its historic center and marvel at the medieval castle overlooking the town. Upon arriving in Turin, return your rental car and spend the afternoon exploring any missed sights or indulging in one last *caffè* before departing.

Tuscan Trails: A Scenic Drive Through Italy's Heartland

Day 1: Arrival in Florence

Begin your Tuscan adventure in **Florence,** the region's cultural capital. After picking up your rental car, spend the day exploring the city's iconic landmarks, including the **Florence Cathedral, Uffizi Gallery,** and **Ponte Vecchio.** Enjoy a leisurely stroll through the historic center, savoring *gelato* from local artisanal shops and soaking in the vibrant atmosphere of this Renaissance gem.

Day 2: Florence to Siena

On day two, set out from Florence and head south towards the medieval city of **Siena,** approximately **70 kilometers** away. Along the way, make a detour to visit the charming hilltop town of **San Gimignano,** known for its iconic medieval towers and scenic vistas. Continue your journey to Siena, where you can wander through narrow cobblestone streets, visit the stunning **Siena Cathedral,** and indulge in Tuscan cuisine at a traditional trattoria.

Day 3: Siena to Montepulciano and Pienza

Embark on a scenic drive through the rolling hills of the **Val d'Orcia**, stopping in the hilltop towns of **Montepulciano** and **Pienza**. Montepulciano is approximately **50 kilometers** from Siena, while Pienza is a further 20 kilometers south. Explore Montepulciano's historic center, renowned for its Renaissance architecture and world-class wines, before continuing to Pienza, a UNESCO World Heritage Site famous for its pecorino cheese. Take time to wander through Pienza's charming streets, visit local cheese shops, and admire panoramic views of the Val d'Orcia from the town's scenic overlooks.

Day 4: Pienza to Montalcino and Val d'Orcia

Continue your journey through the Val d'Orcia, stopping in the medieval town of **Montalcino**, approximately **20 kilometers** from Pienza, known for its prestigious **Brunello di Montalcino** wine. Visit local wineries for tastings of this renowned wine varietal and enjoy a leisurely lunch overlooking the rolling vineyards. In the afternoon, explore the picturesque countryside of the Val d'Orcia, dotted with cypress trees, olive groves, and golden wheat fields, before returning to Pienza for the evening.

Day 5: Pienza to Montecatini Terme

Depart from Pienza and head towards the charming town of **Montecatini Terme**, approximately **200 kilometers away**. Spend the day relaxing in the town's renowned thermal baths, indulging in spa treatments, and exploring the surrounding parklands. Unwind and rejuvenate in the healing waters of Montecatini Terme before retiring for the evening.

Day 6: Montecatini Terme to Lucca

On your final day, depart from Montecatini Terme and make your way to the enchanting city of **Lucca**, approximately **40 kilometers** away. Upon arriving in Lucca, stroll along the city's ancient walls, explore its well-preserved historic center, and marvel at its impressive Renaissance architecture. Conclude your Tuscan road trip with a delicious dinner at a local trattoria, savoring the flavors of this captivating region.

Sicilian Splendors: A Road Trip Itinerary

Day 1: Arrival in Palermo

Begin your Sicilian adventure in the vibrant capital city of **Palermo**. After arriving at the airport, pick up your rental car and head to your accommodation in the heart of the city. Spend the day exploring Palermo's historic center, where you can wander through bustling markets, admire magnificent architecture, and sample traditional Sicilian street food. Don't miss iconic landmarks such as the **Norman Palace, Palermo Cathedral**, and the lively **Ballarò Market**.

Day 2: Palermo to Agrigento

On day two, depart from Palermo and journey southeast towards the ancient city of **Agrigento**, approximately **130 kilometers** away. Along the way, make a stop at the enchanting hilltop town of **Monreale** to visit its stunning Norman cathedral, renowned for its intricate mosaics. Continue your drive to Agrigento, where you can explore the awe-inspiring **Valley of the Temples**, a UNESCO World Heritage Site featuring well-preserved Greek ruins overlooking the Mediterranean Sea.

Day 3 and 4: Agrigento to Syracuse

Continue your journey eastward along the southern coast to **Syracuse**, approximately **250 kilometers** from Agrigento. En route, consider a detour to visit the charming town of **Noto**, known for its Baroque architecture and delicious gelato. In Syracuse, explore the historic island of **Ortygia**, home to ancient ruins, medieval streets, and picturesque piazzas. Don't miss the opportunity to visit the ancient **Greek theater** and the **Ear of Dionysius**. Spend the night in Syracuse.

Day 5: Syracuse to Taormina

Depart from Syracuse and travel north along the coast to **Taormina**, approximately **120 kilometers** away. Upon arriving in Taormina, take a cable car ride up to the town from the coast for breathtaking views of the **Ionian Sea** and **Mount Etna**. Explore the ancient **Greek Theater**, stroll along **Corso Umberto**, and indulge in Sicilian cuisine at a local trattoria. Spend the night in Taormina.

Day 6: Taormina to Catania

Continue your journey north to **Catania**, approximately **50 kilometers** from Taormina. In Catania, explore the bustling **fish market,** visit the **Baroque Cathedral of Saint Agatha,** and wander through the historic streets lined with black lava stone buildings. Don't miss the chance to sample Sicilian street food, including arancini and cannoli. Spend the night in Catania.

Day 6 and 7: Catania to Cefalù

On your final day, depart from Catania and travel west along the northern coast to **Cefalù,** approximately **180 kilometers** away. Along the way, consider a stop in the picturesque seaside town of Cefalù, known for its sandy beaches and **Norman Cathedral.** Explore the historic center, relax on the beach, and enjoy a farewell dinner at a local restaurant.

You can then arrange your trip back from the town of Cefalù to the city of Palermo. It's about a **70-kilometer** drive along the northern coast of Sicily, typically taking around **1 hour and 15 minutes** by car, depending on traffic conditions.

Appendix B – Drive With Children: Italian Laws

As specified on the Aci's (Automobile Club d'Italia) website:
https://www.aci.it/fileadmin/documenti/viaggia_con_noi/pdf/Driving_in_Italy_information_for_visiting_motorists/Carrying.pdf

Carrying Children Safely

Children **up to 1.5 m in height** must always be placed in **an approved restraint system** or seated in a child seat suitable for their weight. Children over 1.5 m in height must wear ordinary adult seat belts.

The driver, or the adult accompanying the minor, is responsible for compliance regarding the use of an appropriate restraint system/child seat or seat belts.

Fine for non-compliance (article 172, paragraph 10, Italian Highway Code): **80 to 323 Euros** (penalty points on Italian driving license: -5 out of 20 full starting points).

Children Transportation Safety Tips

1) The most appropriate child restraint:

- is suitable for the child's weight;

- bears the European type-approval label (ECE R 44-04).

2) Fitting the child restraint properly:

- fully comply with the manufacturer's instructions;
- if the car is equipped with an Isofix system the child restraint is more safely installed, being directly and rigidly attached to the car structure;
- it is forbidden to fit the child restraint rearward facing on the front seat, unless the airbag is turned off.

3) Placing the child correctly in the child restraint:

- make sure that the diagonal belt passes across the child's shoulder rather than neck;
- make sure you fasten seat belts correctly so as to secure the child in the seat.

Please note that a collision at 15 km/h (9.321 mph) can be fatal for a child not secured with appropriate child restraint. In a crash at 56 km/h (34.7984 mph), a child weighing 15 kg (33, 07 lbs.) develops a striking force equal to 225 kg (496, 04 lbs.). No matter how tightly you try to hold the child, he/she would be ripped from your arms.

Road accidents are the first cause of death in Europe for children aged 5 to 13 years old: 12,000 minors die on the roads each year, 5,000 out of them are children.

About 40% of the European children are transported by car without child restraint systems and more than 50% are placed in inadequate devices (that is, not complying with the international standards, not matching the child's weight or wrongly fitted in the vehicle).

Groups of Restraints

Weight / Age	Group	Safest seat for the restraint system	Safest position for the restraint system
Up to 10 kg *about 12 months old*	**Group 0**	Rear seat	Rearward facing
Up to 13 kg *about 24 months old*	**Group 0+**	Rear seat	Rearward facing
9 to 18 kg *9 months to 4 years old*	**Group 1**	Rear seat	Rearward facing, up to 2 years old, if indicated by model instructions. Forward facing for all other models
15 to 25 kg *3 to 6 years old*	**Group 2**	Either front or rear seat	Forward facing
22 to 36 kg *5 to 12 years old*	**Group 3**	Either front or rear seat	Forward facing

Children on Motorcycles

Only one passenger **aged at least 5** can be carried on a motorcycle, provided the child can seat comfortably balanced and wear an EU homologated helmet.

Fine for non-compliance of age limit (article 170, paragraph 6bis, Italian Highway Code): **160 to 641 Euros** (penalty points on Italian driving license: 0 out of 20 full starting points).

Fine for non-compliance of compulsory helmet for the child aged at least 5 (article 171, paragraph 2, Italian Highway Code): **80 to 323 Euros** (penalty points on Italian driving license: -5 out of 20 full starting points).

Appendix C – Most Common Road Signs in Italy

Warning and Regulatory Road Signs

Warning signs in Italy are often red or yellow to advise of potential danger. You should take note of any warning signs in Italy as they are designed to alert you of possible dangers ahead.

STOP AND GIVE WAY	GIVE WAY	CHILDREN CROSSING
TWO WAY TRAFFIC	BEND RIGHT	ROAD WORKS
GIVE PRIORITY TO VEHICLES FROM OPPOSITE DIRECTION	PRIORITY ROAD	ROUNDABOUT AHEAD

Most Common Information Road Signs in Italy

Information signs in Italy are the most frequently used road signs in Italy and are generally used on any type of road to provide road users with general information about the road they are using and the road ahead.

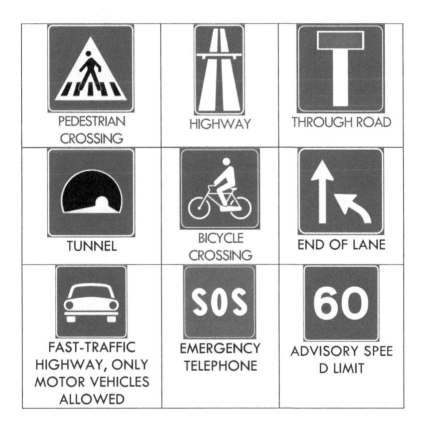

PEDESTRIAN CROSSING	HIGHWAY	THROUGH ROAD
TUNNEL	BICYCLE CROSSING	END OF LANE
FAST-TRAFFIC HIGHWAY, ONLY MOTOR VEHICLES ALLOWED	EMERGENCY TELEPHONE	ADVISORY SPEE D LIMIT

Most Common Mandatory Road Signs in Italy

Mandatory road signs in Italy are used where you are required to carry out a specific task, they are not suggestions, information or advisory signs, they must be adhered to and as such are arguably the most important roads signs in Italy that you need to know.

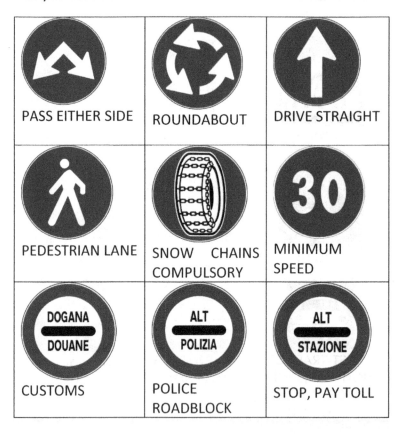

PASS EITHER SIDE	ROUNDABOUT	DRIVE STRAIGHT
PEDESTRIAN LANE	SNOW CHAINS COMPULSORY	MINIMUM SPEED
CUSTOMS	POLICE ROADBLOCK	STOP, PAY TOLL

Prohibitory Road Signs in Italy

Prohibitory road signs in Italy are used on all road types in Italy, often to restrict certain types of vehicles and certain manoeuvres such as prohibiting u-turns or setting maximum speeds.

NO PARKING ON SIDE WHERE SIGN IS PLACED.	NO STOPPING ON THE SIDE WHERE SIGN IS PLACED	RESTRICTED VEHICULAR ACCESS
NO ENTRY FOR VEHICULAR TRAFFIC	NO OVERTAKING	MAXIMUM SPEED 50 KM/H
NO USE OF HORNS	NO VEHICLES OVER WIDTH SHOWN	NO MOTOR VEHICLES WITH FOUR OR MORE WHEELS

Common Words on Road Signs

Here are some words that you'll see on Italian road signs:

entrata → entrance
uscita → exit
servizio → service station (gas)
passo carrabile → keep clear
pedaggio → toll
contanti → cash
carta di credito → credit card
corsia → lane
Autostrada → toll motorway/highway
Dogana → customs
alt stazione → stop to pay toll
deviazione → deviation
raccordo → connection
stazione → station
ospedale → hospital
centro → city center
area pedonale → pedestrian area
ZTL → limited traffic zone
aperto → open
chiuso → closed
solo → only
area successiva → next area
senso unico → one direction
eccetto → except for / excluding

THANK YOU for purchasing and reading my book.

Receive as a gift my short guide: *Etiquette Tips for Dining in Italy*

Download it at:

www.mistralbooks.com/andreaventerra

or scan the QR Code below:

Enjoy reading!

Disclaimer

All content and information in this book, including programs, products, and/or services, are for informational and educational purposes only. It does not constitute professional advice of any kind and does not establish any kind of professional-client relationship. While I strive to provide accurate general information, the information presented here is not a substitute for professional advice, and you should not rely solely on it. Always consult a professional in the relevant area for your particular needs and circumstances before making any professional, legal, or financial decision.

The information contained in this book is published after careful verification of sources, selected with care, and, as far as possible, updated and official. However, it is not possible to guarantee the absence of errors and the correctness of the disclosed information.

The book may include hyperlinks to websites managed by third parties, including advertisements and other content providers. These sites may collect data or request personal information from the user.

The author of this book does not exercise, and is not required to exercise, any form of control and therefore declines any responsibility for damages, claims, or losses, direct or indirect, arising in any form to the user from the viewing, use, and/or functioning of third-party sites or services reached through such links. Therefore, the risks associated with the use of such sites will be entirely the responsibility of the user.

Made in the USA
Las Vegas, NV
16 May 2024

89992601R10059